PUBLISHED BY
Aulsondro "Novelist" Hamilton
Information, Technology, and Literacy Foundation
AULGRAY 31 Media, LLC (U.S.A.)
Emcee N.I.C.E. (U.S.A.)

DESIGNED BY
Aulsondro "Novelist" Hamilton

PRINTED IN THE U.S.A.

ISBN: 978-0-9963703-6-3

Library of Congress Control Number: 2022914184

First Edition: August 2022

AULSONDRO
"NOVELIST"
HAMILTON
A.K.A. EMCEE N.I.C.E.

"In the music business there will be many storms that a professional recording artist goes through to achieve greatness, through the trials, you just have to remember to stay steadfast knowing that there is light on the other side of it, and you will achieve."

- Emcee N.I.C.E.

A message from N.I.C.E. mentors…

"When I was early in my career and earlier in his career, I was blessed to meet and work with a young Novelist. Years later I am inspired by his hustle, drive and success."

- Paul Stewart
Music Supervisor / Music Producer
(2 Fast 2 Furious, Hustle & Flow, Insecure)

"I have never met a guy like Emcee N.I.C.E. who can do it all, this guy can produce, write, rap, market, promote, he is a one stop shop, when I needed anything musically before speaking to Jimmy Iovine, I would call him to get his opinion, I LOVE IT!"

- Kevin Black
Former VP Warner Bros. Records
Former VP of Rap Promotions Interscope Records
(2 Pac, Dr. Dre, Snoop, Eminem, 50 Cent, No Doubt)

"Aulsondro (Novelist) Hamilton: A true industry protege who is accomplishing his goals and aspirations far beyond the pale. He's an entrepreneur, a teacher, a leader and is inspiring in all aspects of entertainment. Live up and stay up."

- Tom McGee
CEO, TMG/StreetPride

"Novelist has always been ahead of his time and he is definitely a wealth of knowledge. When it comes to the music business he is accomplished and a master writer, producer, recording artist, and advocate for creator rights and education."

- Chantal Grayson
CEO, Industry Executive

ACKNOWLEDGEMENT

I am thankful to all of the people that I have met in the music business and all of the years of knowledge and wisdom I gained that has helped me start and curate the Music Release University.

From my mother Debbie Jackson-Mangual may she continue to rest in power, she was my first manager and we had no knowledge about the music business, just that we wanted to be in it and she was like you have to get in it to learn it.

My pops and mentor may he rest in peace **De'Jon J.H. Clark** aka Mr. 30 Minutes early to every meeting who taught me that paying attention to details is key to everything in life, especially the music business. Fear no one, but respect everyone, respect the process and you will command respect. Great leaders develop other leaders.

My first major manager **Paul Stewart** aka DJ P aka White Boy from Compton. When I started with *Lighter Shade of Brown*, I watched how Paul maneuvered and said to myself I want to make moves like this dude. He managed not only Lighter Shade of Brown, but *Coolio, Montel Jordan, Pharcyde,* and many other legends and became the President of Def Jam West. He showed me how to be elusive, smart, and intelligently aggressive with my approach to the game. Which was very instrumental in me putting this series together.

Shiro Gutzie for showing me the blueprint without

showing me the blueprint on how to navigate the industry and become seen so much that you get recognized, he is very strategic in his marketing and approach.

Kevin Black, "Always bet on Black!" Mr. Hype is the King of everything! One of Interscope Records greatest promotional generals, known as one of the modern marketing geniuses to ever do it, from Dr. Dre to Snoop to 2 Pac, Eminem, 50 Cent, The Game, No Doubt, KB could give you a vision, a goal, a plan and would execute it, all you had to do was watch and you learned that hype with a budget mixed with "FOMO" (fear of missing out) can open the world for you, thank you for allowing me to watch and learn.

TMG Street Pride's **Tom McGee** who taught me the value of not only working a record, but positioning a record politically so that you give it every opportunity for it to be successful and it paid off. I thank you Tom for the wisdom that you've bestowed upon me to not only mentally grow and but having the ability to implement it as well. To every group I have been a part of in multiple genres across the board, I thank them. I learn something from every situation that became teachable moments. Every soundtrack, every collaboration all aiding in my thoughts of me carving out this goto guide for artists and I hope it not only shortens your path to success, but helps you sustain it.

Juanita Stephens who showed me the proper way to roll out a record release plan through PR and that any narrative can be redefined where you can "make believers out of non-believers."

Chantal Grayson as a high-level executive in the music industry she taught me that without faith and resources it's just a dream. That it's one thing to have a vision, another thing to do the research, set goals, and a plan- then allocate resources, to make your dreams come to reality.

TABLE OF CONTENTS

INTRODUCTION TO MUSIC RELEASE UNIVERSITY

Music Release University: "The Indies' Guide to Releasing Music Today!" is part of a series of books directed towards independent artists. As an indie artist there is a plethora of content good and bad available concerning writing and recording a record, but very little good information on what to do once your vision has come to fruition. This series of books and my courses address a lot of the questions indie artists have pertaining to their music career. In my opinion, artists just simply need easy to understand information and gain solid guidance on how to properly release a single and or album into the marketplace today.

The series will also highlight potential strategies artists can learn about and how to tweak and implement it right now to overcome various pitfalls they may encounter along their journey or finding their niche and releasing their project.

As an artist just starting out or if you've been at it for a minute but not seeing the results you envision, this book will serve as a great foundation to build on, strengthen your mindset and help you formulate who you are as an artist before the "positions" infiltrate and attempt to dictate the should've, would've, could've in your life. I will further discuss the term "positions" later in this book. The benefits an artist can gain by reading this book are real ways that an artist can be successful and not be inundated by a bunch of "positions" meaning the lawyers, the managers, the booking agents, the contracts, etc...

Although we will touch on those things, that will not be the primary focus of this book in the series "Music Release University: "The Indies' Guide to Releasing Music!" With the knowledge gained from this book you - the artist, will be able to visualize, research, set goals, and execute a plan that is right for you no matter where you are at in your career. Starting with book one - an overview of what you will need to know when you are ready to release your song into the marketplace today.

To be truthful the whole recording process starts with the belief in self! Yup, your mindset is two-thirds of your ability to finish a project and hopefully be one of the few lucky ones to have a long career in the music business.

MRU BREAKDOWN

CLASSES - WHERE DO YOU FIT IN?

FRESHMEN

SOPHOMORE

JUNIOR

SENIOR

1. MRU BREAKDOWN, Where do you fit?

(Your Mindset at each university level will consist of your understanding of the music business when it comes to releasing music)

- FRESHMEN Mindset

Welcome to the Music Release University campus/series. Orientation is pretty simple, hypothetically, you have your acceptance letter, your parents just dropped you off and some stranger greets you at the dormitory, shows you your room and then tells you to meet at the quad at noon where a bunch of vendors are set up to try to allure- I mean invite you to join them. You on the other hand already know you want to be… A recording artist.

So, you've got the VISION, but No real understanding of how the music business works yet. All you can think about is the things you want to do in music and how you are going to take over the whole industry. You have big dreams and big goals but no plan in place, so you try everything, thinking you're in the "know" but you are not, the rookie/freshmen mistake is not properly assessing the industry. This is typical of all freshmen, only in the music business though the stakes are higher - financially, morally, emotionally, and I'll tell you why in phase one and very risky without knowledge.

- SOPHOMORE Mindset

With this mindset, I see you're still here and still interested. I guess you are determined to be a recording artist after all. Now that you know where the chemistry lab is located. Time to test the compounds on the periodic table and see what works well together and what causes irrefutable damage. This is where the RESEARCH happens. You got your feet wet, had some mild success with some things and no response with others. There are several things that take place here when your part of the music industry, starting with the realization that the music business is constantly evolving. With the sophomore mindset, you get a sense of what type of work is going to be expected from you to take your chosen profession to the next level and who some of the players are. This is pivotal because aside from the evolution of the music business you've also come to realize that between 30,000 to 60,000 thousand songs a day are being released, that is 720,000 songs a year (yes, a whole lot of music being released). Upon further research, you discover that only 100,000 artists will really make any money off of their music and out of the 100k only 800 of those songs have any real potential of being a breakout hit. (Via Spotify)

Then your research guides you to dig deeper, and you realize that anybody can go viral, but how do you stay consistent and relevant? How does viral convert to profit? This is called conversion.

(**Side bar:** What does it mean to go viral? Does virality equal success in the music business with so many artists having viral moments versus longevity?)

If you don't know, the answer will come when you

lay the foundation after understanding that freshman mindset.

So, I ask you again, do you want to be famous, or do you want to be rich, and make music to inspire…?

Equipped with a whole new determination and focus, kick yourself into overdrive because the wins are coming. Time to set some GOALS and make a solid PLAN to execute your vision.

- **JUNIOR** Mindset

Hey now you're a big person - notice I didn't use a pronoun, on campus. Walking through the quad people notice you and they know what you are all about. You're the campus recording artist, the next Grammy winner and on tour selling out arenas all over the world type of artist.

Sorry I got a head of myself, remember the music business is constantly evolving so you are living the dream but one day you wake up and realize you are late for your final, you rush over to the chemistry lab and the doors are closed. Oh, my bad, you didn't get the intra campus email saying the final was moved to the international building on the other side of the campus. But wait you were settled in, now you must pivot but because you now know the following, you will be okay:

a.   You know, what does & does not work for you.
b.   You've had some major wins

6

c.	You now have a real understanding of your brand and marketing,
d.	You now know how radio works, how venues work, how you work and what works well with your voice,
e.	You know what music fits you
f.	You know what trends are happening and more…

With your newfound knowledge of self, when the powers that be move the measure of success goal post, instead of freaking out you adjust *(trust me, they are going to move them)*. Luckily, you know where the international building is and you make it over there right before they close the door to take your final exam. At this point you are well equipped mentally, physically, emotionally, and most definitely spiritually, you now know what the industry wants as you ponder the direction to move for your career by adding tweaks to your plan.

Sidebar: Until there is a full understanding of the freshmen mindset, with the sophomore mindset, you will not get here, every goal, benchmark, and process needs to have the same sense of urgency and level of deep understanding prior to moving on. This is exactly why I've combined the sophomore/junior mindset. It's sort of like college when you finally are over the prerequisites and get to dive deeper into your field of interest and take courses that pertain specifically to what you want to get your degree in, remember success is about having the knowledge.

- **SENIOR** Mindset

With this mindset, it feels so good to have a lot of knowledge. How convenient for you going into this phase of your career. Your team is irreplaceable at this point and comprises a handful of skilled professionals. You have learned the value of relationships by now and you are grateful that your roomies knew you when you were just getting your feet wet full of dreams and aspirations. What you do now will determine your longevity in the music business. You've made it into the 100k club breaking through and making money off your music. At this point you are a star on the verge, you've taken your VISION, fleshed it out with some RESEARCH, set some GOALS and executed a full PLAN and because you were diligent and dedicated to the process you are now winning bigtime, the next move from here is becoming a star. At this point it's like you've graduated, and it is now time to embark upon the journey you've cultivated over the last four years (metaphorically speaking). This isn't an overnight success story as many would want you to believe. No this is a sacrifice and an intelligently structured plan being realized. The day after you receive your degree you become an alumnus of MRU.

What becomes of your music career now is in your hands.

- **MASTERS** Mindset

You've become a star...
This is for the last book in the series.

PHASE ONE
VISION

2.   PHASE ONE - YOU'RE A FRESHMAN

VISION

Visualize what you want to achieve with your project and be realistic, especially if you have a small and or limited budget and limited relationships. Now if you have tangible relationships that can help your prevail in the music business, you will still have to ask yourself are you willing to lose those relationships if you leverage them on a project they may not be confident and or interested in? (Just because you believe don't mean others do) Also depending on who the investor is, they may only want to see the numbers and be indifferent to why you are trying to be a professional recording artist. When money comes into play, you must ask yourself some tough questions prior to embarking on your musical journey. If you opt to skip a class, take it from someone who has been in the music business as an artist to a high-level music executive, not paying your dues is a complete mistake. You have to look in the mirror and have that real conversation with yourself.

Ask yourself, do you want to be famous, or do you want to be rich? One requires social activity, being constantly visible and constantly active. While the other forces you to home in on what makes an artist a star, whether it's musically, from a marketing standpoint, just a full forensic breakdown of success, learning the genetics of superstardom, the research and then cultivating the sound with the focus on establishing you as not only an artist, but as a brand.

Through my journey in the music business, I have met countless artists that have no real ideal and or understanding of all the phases of the music business. Or they have been misguided by parts and pieces that they've picked up along the way or been given to by people they believe are in the know, yet they don't have the whole roadmap to be successful. Then they come to find that to execute the information that they were given, there are a few other things that need to happen.

In the process of discovering myself, I have tapped into many genres of music from Hip Hop to Alternative Rap to R&B Hip Hop, to Urban Rock back to hip hop to finally landing my purpose as a Christian Hip Hop artist in a genre called CHH otherwise known as Christian Hip Hop.

Yes it took me a little minute, but hey, I got here and now I am giving the shortcut to you from my blueprint.

The beauty about going through the vision process, is figuring out your end game and then reverse engineering that vision to achieve the outcome you wish to have through the steps that you will need to focus on to achieve the level of success in which you seek. Let's brainstorm together!

Below I've provided a Venn Diagram for the visualization brainstorming session you are about to have.

Below is the Venn Diagram.

(A Venn diagram uses overlapping circles or other shapes to illustrate the logical relationships between two or more sets of items. Often, they serve to graphically organize things, highlighting how the items are similar and different.)

In the top circle define what happiness means to you, in the bottom left circle write down being rich and in the bottom right circle write down what's your definition of famous and how you see yourself living. The overlapping circles are all the things that are common among the outer circles. With the vision, as you visualize you should also analyze self and ask yourself the following:

ARTIST

- Do you know who you are?
- Do you know who you are as a recording artist?
- What's your story?
- What makes you unique?
- Music is meant to release and inspire; how will you inspire?

GENRE

Before you can define your music by genre, you must ask yourself these important questions:

- Do you know what a genre of music is?
- What genre would you like to be a part of?
- Is it possible to be a part of several genres?

- What defines that genre of music? (For example, rap today is known for the 808 drum and melodic vibes.) What style of music do you want to do?
- Does that style fit your voice and persona?

I'm certain you've seen or heard of American Idol™ or The Voice™ on network television.

These shows show the viewer great examples of an artist selecting the wrong song for their vocal range and style. The audience knows immediately if that artist can sing or not. The unfortunate part is that you are now being measured against the great versus yourself. There is nothing worse than your mic going out or missing a dance cue in front of an in-person arena that all have their camera ready to capture your highs and of course your lows. Often the wrong selection of music resulted in the artist being sent home. In this case you only have one shot. Thank goodness that in life as long as you have more time and knowledge, you can make adjustments and try different genres. I don't recommend making your preliminary choices public because sometimes you must work twice as hard to re-brand and market yourself once the public has a certain perspective of who you are as an artist.

An extra sheet is provided with the Venn Diagram just in case you need more space.

VENN DIAGRAM: "This is where you brainstorm *Phase One: Visualization*

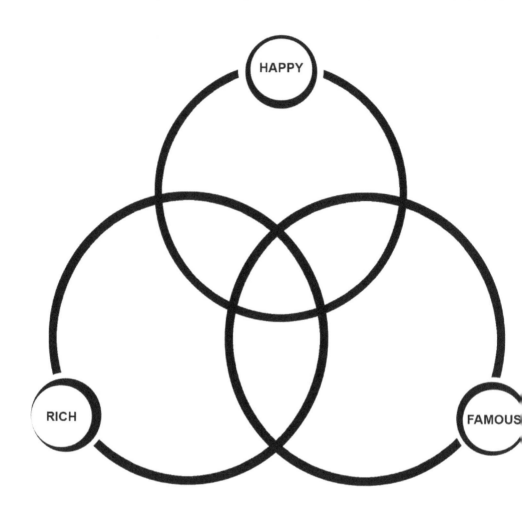

VENN DIAGRAM: *Phase One: Visualization* continued.

HAPPY   RICH   FAMOUS

_____ _____ _____

_____ _____ _____

_____ _____ _____

_____ _____ _____

_____ _____ _____

_____ _____ _____

_____ _____ _____

_____ _____ _____

_____ _____ _____

_____ _____ _____

_____ _____ _____

_____ _____ _____

_____ _____ _____

OVERLAP 1   OVERLAP 2   CENTER   OVERLAP 3

_____ _____ _____ _____

_____ _____ _____ _____

_____ _____ _____ _____

_____ _____ _____ _____

_____ _____ _____ _____

_____ _____ _____ _____

Now to one of my favorite techniques...

S.W.O.T.

If you've followed my career or not, one of the things that I am extremely passionate about is a business process called S.W.O.T. in which stands for **Strengths, Weaknesses, Opportunities,** and **Threats**. I personally S.W.O.T. everything and I mean, everything when it comes to the music business, not only my business endeavors but my life. So, let's do the first part of S.W.O.T together. Below is a survey - again do not skip classes or assignments because you will really need these micro lessons to build your dream career in the recording industry.

STRENGTHS & WEAKNESSES

What are your strengths and weaknesses in the following areas? Please be honest with yourself, this is all about your growth as an artist and if you can't be real with you, stop now. Give yourself a rating from 1 to 5 with 1 being the weakest and 5 being the strongest.

(Circle One)

   1. Singing/Rapping Experience

       1 2   3   4   5

   2. Songwriting/Song Structure Experience

       1   2   3   4   5

3. Real Live Performance Experience

    1   2   3   4   5

4. Production Experience

    1   2   3   4   5

5. Play any instruments

    1   2   3   4   5

6. Understanding of Engineering/Mastering

    1   2   3   4   5

7. Understanding of Marketing

    1   2   3   4   5

8. Understanding of Branding

    1   2   3   4   5

9. Knowledge of your consumers/audience

    1   2   3   4   5

10. Understanding of Management

    1   2   3   4   5

11. Understanding of Split Sheets

    1   2   3   4   5

12. Understanding of Agreements/Contracts

    1   2   3   4   5

13. Your understanding of music distribution

    1   2   3   4   5

14. Radio Experience

    1   2   3   4   5

15. You know who the genre influencers are

    1   2   3   4   5

16. Understand Social Media

    1   2   3   4   5

17. Familiar with the latest technology in music

    1   2   3   4   5

If you've answered 5 to all these music related points, Congratulations! You don't need to keep reading this book, you already have all the answers and I expect to see your shining star on a Grammy ballot and red carpets. The Recording Academy aka The Grammys and or Grammy awards nominee, nomination and win is the pinnacle in an artists' career.

Now for the rest of you, by looking at your answers, it will reveal to you areas that will be your focus areas, directly related to your growth. That's why being honest with yourself, and your answers are so critical to you being able to win and answering the questions above is designed to give you a thorough understanding of your strengths and weaknesses so that you can fortify your knowledge in which makes you a better artist and one that can adapt. Let's not forget the goal here is to not skip any portion of the S.W.O.T. process.

Moving on to the O and T in which stands for Opportunities and Threats. S.W.O.T. is a basic business principle, but I recommend that you should make S.W.O.T. applicable to not only your business but your life as well. Again, there is no separation of indie artists and business. All indie artists, welcome to the music business!

Can you identify an opportunity or a threat when it comes to releasing your music?

Is radio an opportunity or a threat?

Is social media an opportunity or a threat?

Are you an opportunity or a threat?

Are distro platforms opportunities or threats?

Knowledge is not only power, it's how you survive in a killer whale eats killer whale world.

NOTES

In the next few chapters, we are going to dive into your mindset, S.W.O.T., and of course releasing a record or album. Take notes and be sure to participate in the exercises I have created throughout the book.

DEFINE YOUR BRAND

Your brand is the image consumers have of you as an artist, so defining it is one of the most important things you will have to do, or the market (consumers, journalists, haters) will do it for you.

1. What will your brand stand for?
2. Do you have a mission?
3. Will you be cause driven?
4. Will it align with your core beliefs and values?
5. Will you have an understanding of the trends and the ability to shift the message?
6. Do you know the difference between sales and branding?
7. Every Brand needs a plan.

Your #1 goal as an indie artist or reestablishing artist and or business, is growth and sustainability and your moves should be clear, dedicated, and focused at all levels.

Once your VISION is fleshed out then it's on to the RESEARCH and setting GOALS that will be needed to bring that vision to fruition in PHASE TWO.

PHASE TWO
RESEARCH
GOALS

3.   PHASE TWO RESEARCH & GOALS

Visualize what you want to achieve with your project and be realistic, and when I mean be realistic, that doesn't mean you can release a song and or album with no understanding and plan because that will leave you disappointed and all you will have is just a record sitting on the shelf that no one cares about, well maybe your cousins and friends, but that's not going to get you on the charts and or position for any one of those popular awards. Not to mention, a waste of money because it cost money to record and release a record / album.

For example, artists are constantly asking me for record impact advice - which I often give only to tune into the news within my genre and realize that the same artists that asked for advice released a single and then a few weeks, not even months released a second single. Or worse, an artist is getting some momentum with a single and instead of further investing into that single they immediately drop another record- thus killing the momentum of the first record. This is not the type of career where more is better. Not to mention depending on the region you live in or where you are releasing your record, all of that matters and can determine the overall success of the project.

There are plenty of artists that are known in one region (market) and oblivious in another.

- RESEARCH

After you have visualized what you want to be, do and where you want to go with your project, now the research happens. At this point you now have an introductory or shall I say preliminary understanding of how the music industry moves prior to fully immersing yourself in the business of making and releasing records. You must go beyond the surface of a simple Google search and hearsay.

The research happens with understanding who the players are in your field and knowing that these positions change often, so any move that must be made on your part, must be made quickly after crafting a well thought out plan to increase the likelihood of your success. There is nothing like being in the know, with facts, it makes your navigation much simpler and easy. It will also help you put together a budget that will help make your plan easier to implement. NOTHING IS FREE, even FREE isn't FREE you will need a realistic honest budget *(Not what you are going to get, it's what you have at your immediate disposal)* and if you cannot be honest with yourself regarding your budget by which I mean the *funds to invest in your project / career*, then you have already "capped" out and lost. To "cap" for those of you not familiar with the term means to be fake and, in this situation, it makes absolutely no sense to cap yourself, when it's your livelihood at stake.

Half the battle is being in the know of what's needed to be successful and that is having a plan and setting goals is the other half of what it takes to achieve your goals.

After the research, you should know who you are… as an artist, brand, and what the consumer wants. Yes, up to this point we have been focusing on you, but part of winning is knowing your audience. For example, if you are a country or rock artist you should know the value of open mic and touring local gigs. It's in the rock n roll DNA to perform at local bars and clubs. You should know your strengths and weaknesses and have not only an objective but an end goal. Know what you want out of your release.

GOALS

Now that you know what you want to do, it's time to set "Achievable Goals" and what is meant by that, is to set little goals to achieve that will springboard you to the bigger goals.

For instance, if your objective is to:
Sell Records
Shoot a Music Video
Get on Radio/Streaming
Get on the Charts
Become Rich and Famous

There is a great book I highly recommend that helps explain how little actions lead to big results. *"The Slight Edge" by Jeff Olson.* The premise of the book is that simple daily choices can shape your success and overall happiness. Throughout my book I am also indirectly going to be elaborating on not only releasing records how-to but on ways to strengthen your mindset whether via book recommendations or mediation.

We know becoming rich and famous doesn't happen without the 4 objectives prior to that, so that would be the last goal, and this is also based on the budget you have put together to achieve them. If you didn't catch the key word in that last sentence, it was budget. Yes, we need to talk about that too. And, I'm not saying that you need a lot of money, but relationships will only take you so far. Professional people make a living being a professional i.e., expert in what they do. They will not work for free. Once you are done with the fun part (writing and recording) it's time to seek some professionals and incorporate them into your success plan. For example, mixing and mastering costs, radio promoters costs, branding and marketing costs. Not to be discouraging if you don't have any money, I'd recommend you continue to hone your skills until you do have some disposable income. Another thing that I will touch upon is the nickel-n-dime companies and let me tell you there are a ton of them out there that will take your money (budget) and blow it on low conversion/ momentum building paths. It may not seem like a lot but a $30 membership or $9.99 a month subscription adds up and before you know it you've spent thousands of dollars with little to no results. This is frustrating and often leads to an indie artist quitting before they've even had a chance to work a record.

However, before you can do any of those goals, you must handle the business of the song and or album first (this is for the independents), any pro label should have these things moving for you and that involves the following:

NOTE: YOU WILL NEED A PRE-ARTIST CHECKLIST before releasing your record. The checklist can be found in the tools section of this book, Please DO NOT SKIP TO THE TOOLS SECTION being impatient, it will not be beneficial, this is not microwavable information, there will be no sustainable success without going through the processes.

Pro level advice - once the suits (professionals) get involved, you must have thick skin because you can be shelved, meaning a label can just sit on your music and never put it out. If and or when that happens, you're just stuck until they release you or the regime there gets fired which often leads to the new suits working with you or releasing you. Unfortunately, often it's the latter - they release you. As a signed artist, you will be told what to do and when you can and cannot release music. So if you are one of those artists that likes to release a record every two weeks (exaggerating but you know what I mean) - nobody or no label in their right mind will invest hundreds of thousands and or in some cases millions of dollars in you as an artist and let you drop records haphazardly, knowing the climate of how much it actually cost to release a song and or album properly.

When I was VP at a mid-major label, the budget that was needed to release one song for an artist was insane. The campaigns also were like 8 to 12 weeks when breaking an artist, anyway, back to the business of releasing your indie record/album.

Each record needs to be properly documented and by that, I mean proper credit needs to be issued/distributed and negotiated upfront and in writing. Yes, the distribution of credits is negotiable based on everyone's participation in the compilation. I strongly recommend getting the business out of the way first so that you can have some fun creating your project. It doesn't matter who it is, none of this, "oh that's my friend, cousin, sister's best friend's second cousin and I trust them to do what's right" but yet if the record takes off i.e. goes viral or becomes a hit and no agreement upfront, it could be a nightmare nobody can predict a hit record.

So, you're asking how I protect myself and keep my relationships on a good note. Tada in comes the split sheet.

SPLIT SHEETS
with a (One Stop embedded in it)

NOTE: "ONE STOP" – a "one stop" clearance, means someone who is trying to license my song, only has to contact one party to clear both the Master and Publishing Rights.

As an artist who has music in over a dozen motion pictures and made for television soundtracks, I know the feeling of missing a financial opportunity because in the early days I relied on the friend of a friend and could not get a hold of the friend of a friend to get a clearance to place my record in a movie. Now-a-days prior to any record, album or feature I get my split sheet and if it is my record everybody involved must sign off on the one stop so that I am able to send the record to sync licensing company. This does not only pertain to singers, rappers or talent it also pertains to producers, engineers, mixers, masters, writers, anyone that breathed on your project that will claim any percentage of interest in your work of art.

A. A "Split Sheet" is a sheet that should be filled out at the end of a recording session between the songwriters and producer detailing the percentage split of the ownership of the song while everyone is kumbaya, this also includes "publishing" and "writers" information. Usually, a split sheet has the writer's information on it and the publishing information as well.

NOTE: IF YOU DO NOT HAVE A WRITER'S AFFILIATION OR PUBLISHING AFFILIATION THEN YOU NEED TO SET ONE UP EITHER THROUGH BMI, ASCAP, AND OR SESAC. A LIST OF THE PROS WILL BE IN THE TOOLS SECTION WITH LINKS TO THEM.

What is Music Publishing? Music publishing is the business of promotion and monetization of your music: music publishers (BMI, ASCAP and SESAC or SOCAN in Canada just to name a few Performing Rights Organizations (PRO) ensure that songwriters receive royalties for their compositions, and work to generate opportunities for those compositions to be performed and reproduced.

In your split sheet do not forget to add a "one stop clearance" clause, you will thank me for later.

I run across artists all the time that have one or the other, publishing and or writing but they are two separate things. You need a company for both in order for the PRO to collect your royalty for both writers and publishing.

Write down 3 possible names for your writers and publishing company prior to registering with a PRO.

NOTES

Question: How does the PRO know where, when and who to contact to collect your money? Great question- every record prior to release should have an ISRC code embedded in the record. The ISRC code is your digital fingerprint and will automatically ping every time your record is played. No ISRC code, no money, no residual money. What Is An ISRC Code? An International Standard Recording Code (ISRC) is a 12-character, alphanumeric code that is assigned to a piece of music set for commercial release.

The code allows the right(s) holder (that's you and everybody you listed on the split sheet)– whether it's an independent artist or major record label, to identify and track the 'life' of their recording. Ok yes I said life, meaning records that I did 20 years ago are still generating sleep money in the form of residual income. This is the true definition of passive income. Residual income for those of you that don't know is earning that continues after the initial work has been done. In the tools section there is a link to ISRC so that you can get your own ISRC codes.

B. A "One Stop" gives you "the artist" permission to represent the song's interest when it comes to sync licensing. So for instance if you are shopping your song for motion picture, tv, gaming, etc... then a "One Stop" will allow you to secure the placement without having to track down the writers, everyone involved would be cut a check.

C. Getting the "Split Sheet" is very essential for an artist, trust me, it will save you from the drama of having to find everyone involved to sign off.

Unless you produced and wrote everything, then I would still do a split sheet and archive it.

NOTE: PROTECT THE BRAND that is you, make sure all of your paperwork is together. This equals peace of mind. Nobody can predict a hit so protect yourself upfront!

CONTRACTS FOR PRODUCTION
(Unless you've produced it yourself)

A. For every song you do, make sure there is a written agreement between you and the producer that outlines the details of the song and lists who the producer(s) are. It sets out the terms and conditions under which a producer will create music, film or other creative works for their clients. A Producer Agreement is a legal contract between a producer and the artist. If you want to make money off of your music do not buy leased beats because they are generally not exclusive, and the rights belong to the producer not you. It is not authentic to hear on the radio records with the same production. Not to mention many radio stations Program Directors (PD's) frown upon such a practice. If you are curious about how music gets selected and played on the radio, well that is another book-in-itself. For now, just know that the PD is the main gatekeeper to radio and radio play. Part of your music release journey is to get to know the PDs in your area and region for starters before branching out nationally and globally.

B. The agreements cover, services, royalty, publishing, sample clearance, advances / fees (if any), compensation, and whatever's customized.

Notes - What radio stations play your genre of music and who are the PD's in your local area or region.

NOTES

SONGWRITERS COLLABORATION AGREEMENT
(Unless you've written it yourself)

The songwriter collaboration agreement is where the artist and songwriter(s) agree to collaborate. In the agreement are the collaboration details such as the songwriting splits, royalties, publishing splits, expected release date (if available), pretty much everything an artist(s) will need to make sure he/or she is legally protected.

NOTE: YOU "WILL NOT" GET ON THE CHARTS, RECEIVE ROYALTIES, OR SET YOURSELF UP TO WIN, IF YOUR BRAND ISN'T PROTECTED.

AFTER THE RESEARCH
After your research, if you've done it right, then you should have a complete understanding of the following:

As an **ARTIST**
- Know who you are.
- Know who you are as an artist.
- You will have a story
- You will know what makes you unique.
- You will know how you will inspire.
- You will know what you care about, not as an "artist", but as a person.
- You will know if you can be transparent.
- You will know what first impression or second impression you want to make.
- You will (in today's market) understand that you will need to be vulnerable. The advent

of social media dictates your accessibility to your audience.

GENRE
- You will know your Genre.
- You will know if that Genre is viable in the marketplace.
- You will know its strengths and weaknesses.
- You will know what style of music you want to do.
- You will know what fits your voice.

A prime example of knowing your voice is evident on reality shows like The Voice™ and American Idol™ where the wrong song choice has sent many talented singers and artists home for selecting the wrong record and unfortunately their voice did not live up to expectations. I find this incredibly sad because some of the contestants can really sing or rap but the record was wrong.

The flip side is many non-victorious competitors have gone on to have very successful music careers because they knew themselves and their musical strengths and were able to share with the world what they have to offer prior to being eliminated from the reality show. Talent is talent but exposure is king. If the reality route is in your line of sight, be sure to read your contract many artists exchange the exposure for recording 360 deals. In my master's class I cover 360 deals. Are they good for artists in today's market?

STRENGTHS AND WEAKNESSES

- Singing/Rapping Experience
- Songwriting/Song Structure Experience
- Real Live Performance Experience
- Production Experience
- Play any instruments
- Understanding of Engineering/Mastering
- Understanding of Marketing
- Understanding of Branding
- Knowledge of your consumers/audience
- Understanding of Management
- Understanding of Split Sheets
- Understanding of Agreements/Contracts
- Your understanding of music distribution
- Understanding of Radio
- Understanding of Streaming
- Understanding of Sales, Views and Streams
- You know who the influencers are for your genre
- Social Media Presence
- Familiarity with the latest technology concerning music

YOUR REGION

- You will know the music scene in your region for your genre.
- You will know the radio stations.
- You will know the dj's.
- You will know the venues.

- You will know who the other artists are in the region.
- You will know all of the outlets available in your region.

YOUR BRAND

- You will know what your brand will stand for.
- You will know if it will be cause driven.
- You will know your core beliefs and values.
- You will have an understanding of trends and the ability to shift the message.

CONSUMER STUDIES

- You will know who people compare you to.
- You will know who your competitors are.
- You will know who your influences are.
- You will know what your fanbase will look like.
- You will know what fans care about.
- You will understand your future audience
- You will know the demographics in your area.
- You will understand the consumer habits of your genre.
- You will know what social platforms your fans gather on
- You will know how to market to your fans and make new fans.
- You will know your end goal.

This list is very comprehensive and if you are unsure about "any" of the above take a moment to figure out the answer to the above-mentioned attributes. I cannot express the importance of each section I have listed above. There is an opportunity for you in this business no genre is over saturated if you can add value and are talented. Music is the universal language with billions of people seeking and listening daily. Be intentional!

NOTES

PHASE THREE
THE PLAN

4.   PHASE THREE - THE PLAN STEP 1

Now that you have done the research and have outlined the goals along with protecting your brand, it's time to put in place step one of three of phase three.

With this first plan, you will set "Achievable Goals" that keep you moving forward no matter what. We all experience setbacks. Your job is to overcome them in a timely manner and as discreetly as possible and keep your career pushing forward. You must be able to handle what and who people coined "haters", people that don't necessarily want what you have but don't want you to have it either. As "They" say misery loves company. If you've made it this far clearly there is favor in your corner. Be strong and mentally prepared.

What is meant by that, is that you will set little goals to achieve, that will springboard you to the bigger goals.

Remember the book I've recommended helps you develop a success mindset. This is two thirds of your success journey. For instance, look at all of the research that you have done.

Have you created a checklist for everything that needs to be part of your successful music release plan?

Have you established a priority list from the checklist to help you achieve the small victories? If not, take a moment to do so now.

NOTES

Start with the "Artist" category and then move on to each category afterwards. When the boxes are checked, you know that progress is being made. But don't and I mean DO NOT, check the box unless you are 100% certain you have completed it. Hypothetically speaking if you have check boxes for the sake of checking boxes you will get only so far and possibly hurt mentally, financially, and emotionally. This is not a nurturing business. Nurturing, to care for and encourage the growth and development of something. Prior to the music business of today major labels used to have divisions of genuine people that cared about the artist called Artist Developers. They still exist but not like the good old days. Artists are generally young and grow up by the industry instead of in the industry with guidance. Shock value often destroys the human being behind the music we love.

With the checklist you should be able to create little goals that will keep you focused on the tasks. As you check them off, not only will you accomplish many things pertaining to your development, but you will be closer to becoming who you knew you could be.

FRESHMEN - The New Artist Plan

As each category began to get completed, your confidence level will spike because you will be in the know of what it takes to be successful on all levels. Yes, there are levels to this. The *Freshman mindset* does not only apply to new artists. Some artists reading this book are transitioning from being signed to being independent. Being signed is not the only way to have a successful music career now-a-days due to social media and independent distribution channels.

Earlier in the book I described the Music Release University class structures, the first plan is geared towards new artists or newly independent artists we call "freshmen" the new artist plan phase one breaks down like this:

Wait! Before we go there, Have you done the research and established your goals yet? If not, don't continue and get that done first. Don't cheat yourself for real, for real. That's an immediate NO.

NEW ARTIST PLAN

This is after you have researched and set goals, if you have bypassed that, you've already done yourself a disservice. Do all the steps even if you think you are advanced and just want to get to the literal plan. FYI... If you don't know you inside and out, musically, then no plan will make sense or work towards achieving your goals. Your career may fail, you may fail to achieve the goals you had in mind or worse you lack the preparedness you need to prevent you from giving up.

As a new artist not being prepared means you stay a brand-new artist and unknown to any major outlets, radio, DJ's and or Venues. All of which you need to be properly compensated for your music.

The New Indie Artist Plan - should include your budget, and your artist visibility digital presence, musically, visually, and socially. Building a successful artist brand means to be organized and structured, while being organic and authentic. Some of the biggest stars in the music business that you thought were organic, are by design (by professionals), they were coached or developed to form rapport with the consumer. Professionally coached artists are coached to be personable so that the consumer can support them.

Professionally developed artists typically go along with a predetermined plan and because there's often large sums of money involved that the powers that be, put in place that want you to win.

The plan laid out in this book is to help you- the indie artist to construct measurable tasks leading up to a comprehensive plan to help you achieve your goals of being a professional recording artist - someone that gets paid and makes a living from their art. It may look like a lot which is why I broke it down into classes. Either way try to keep it simple enough so that you do not become so overwhelmed. You don't really need to overdo it, your main goal here is to:

a.   Create and Identity.

Start to build the persona that is going to reflect you and your music. The tools above help you formulate this bullet point.

b.   Build a team.

Find a producer, a songwriting partner if needed, an engineer that can not only tap into your sound but knows you and your sound, a photographer / videographer and someone efficient in graphic design that can help pull off your persona. First impressions matter! Social media is a permanent timeline of your evolution. Even if you delete your entire profile someone somewhere may have screen captured your posts so be cognizant of your marketing from day one.

c.   Discover your sound.

Prior to your first release or subsequent release as an indie artist you should have tested the genres. The beauty about discovery is that you are afforded the ability to think outside the box and create. Try different beats and melodies to discover you.

d.   Establish yourself as an artist.

Establishing yourself as an artist simply means to make sure you develop your look and your sound, your identity, your brand. In today's market no matter what you look like, you have an opportunity to be in front of the camera and the face of your music. Labels no longer dictate the look of the talent we see on camera or on stage.

e.   Find out what works well for you.

Another great thing about discovery is that you find out what works well for you. Like the type of microphone that your voice sounds good on. Yes, even the microphone matters. Different mics have different compression which alter the way your voice output sounds.

f.   Figure out what your brand is.

This goes back to the research you did on self, your likes and dislikes. What you want and don't want. Fashion, color schemes, your musical identity. Having a professional photo(s) will set you apart from someone that just took photos on their phone. When you start getting press, having a set of professional photos will be pivotal in your career. Magazines still have quality standards-resolution, brand placements, etc… to consider prior to publishing anything physically or digitally. Copyright becomes a major issue depending on the publisher. I recommend neutral backgrounds with no other prominent brands visible. Also match your look to the season. If you are doing a publication in the summer in California, you should not be wearing a heavy coat as it contrasts with the season and often confuses the intended reader (consumer).

g.   Make sure that you are registered with various platforms.

As a professional recording artist, your digital footprint matters. The more you pop up in search engines the more people take you seriously.

Social Media Registration: *MUA
Facebook 2.9 billion   YouTube 2.2 billion
WhatsApp 2 billion   Instagram 2 billion
WeChat 1.26 billion   TikTok 1 billion
Sina Weibo 573 million   QQ 538.91 million
Telegram 550 million   Snapchat 538 million
Kuaishou 519.8 million   Qzone 517 million
Twitter 436 million   Reddit 430 million

Genius (Lyrics) 100 million

Social media numbers are constantly changing, and they seem to be going in an upward trajectory. As new platforms emerge like the new "kids" on the block TikTok and Clubhouse (although new, these platforms are emerging as two of the premium platforms that you should consider being a part of). No need to worry whether you should or shouldn't because these are the times that we are living in and social media is our new form of communication. Even Madison Ave, the advertising capital of the world has taken notice and now spends a considerable amount of major brands advertising budget on social media influencers and artists.

*MUA = Monthly Active Users

Streaming Registration and Current Payouts
(as of publication):

Tidal, Apple Music, Spotify, Amazon Music, YouTube Music, Pandora, Deezer, Soundcloud, MixCloud.

Here are the current payouts for the Top 7 Streaming services.

Company	*PPS	*STM$1000 Dollars
Tidal	$0.013	76,924 (Streams)
Apple Music	$0.010	100,000 (Streams)
Youtube Music	$0.008	125,000 (Streams)
Deezer	$0.0064	156,250 (Streams)
Amazon Music	$0.0040	250,000 (Streams)

Spotify	$0.0033	303,030	(Streams)
Pandora	$0.0013	769,231	(Streams)

*PPS = Pay Per Stream
*STM = Streams needed to Make $1000 dollars.

This is not a per click payout breakdown, your music must actually play for .30 seconds or more for it to actually count as a stream. It would also be wise to add YouTube ads that incorporate your music that will also add to your streams.

Video Streaming Registration
(as of publication):

YouTube, Vimeo, TikTok, DailyMotion, Wistia, Twitch, Sprout Video, IGTV, Metacafe, Veoh, and Dtube

Here are the current payouts for the Top 7 Video Streaming services.

Company	*PPV	*VVTM $1000 Dollars
Youtube	$3 to $5	200 to 333 (Ad Views)
Twitch	$3.50	286 (Ad Views)
Daily Motion	$1.00	1000 (Ad Views)
Vimeo	$0.26	4,000 (Ad Views)
Vevo	$0.007	100,000 (Ad Views)

*PPV = Pay Per View
*VVTM = Video Views needed to Make $1,000.

Tap into this and other freemium (free) platforms that will help you leave a digital footprint on Google, Bing, Safari and Yahoo (search engine).

h. **Make sure you have a website with a store** (merchandise)

"A website" is not a landing page from a bunch of people's platforms. You can get some of that digital currency by having consumers and fans visit your site and then they could be redirected from there to your other social media platforms. Again, let your personal website be the hub so you can take advantage of monetization opportunities.

Why merch is important:

It would take 3,000 music streams to match revenue from 1 CD sale and 5,000 streams to match revenue from one T-shirt sale *(read that again)*. A lot more artists are making more money selling merch than they are with their music. Not to mention bundling so they sell their music with merch.

The most popular merchandise being sold today are hard goods like T-shirts, mugs, water bottles, posters. Soft goods include items like digital posters, calendars, ringtones etc.

What type of merchandise do you currently have?

NOTES

SOPHOMORE & JUNIORS
The More Established Indie Artist Plan

Ah, with a Sophomores / Juniors mindset, the Music Release University combined these classes due to the level in which people learn and how drastic the initial outcome can be if an artist gets extremely lucky and finds themselves in the right place at the right time with the right record. The following plan is geared towards semi-established to breakout artists we call "Sophomore and Juniors". The established artist plan phase one breaks down like this:

Established Artist Plan
Established indie artist for the purposes of this book defined as you've had success with some major outlets, and radio is somewhat familiar with your artistry. Now you want to expand your reach and presence via campaign runs and radio servicing.

On the other hand, you may have had mild success but no major breakout, you are still unknown to the major outlets, radio and venues. But now you need "focused" marketing and radio servicing.

The Established Artist Plan - This plan is a bigger budget plan because you as the artist has already been in the presence of some radio, you've performed at a few venues or events, but now you're in need of "proper radio servicing" to saturate your product, starting with the surrounding areas of where you're from. Artists you have to capture homebase first.

To further enhance your development, start with better visuals, with marketing support, perform at bigger venues and possibly jump on a tour or start one. Artists and managers should evaluate the analytics of the artists' previous release(s). This will help you gauge where the warm markets are for you and help organize a campaign around your project/tour.

Reaching for the next level in this industry always comes with new objectives. Now that you can confidently say that you have achieved your initial benchmarks. You must set new ones. The main goal here is to:

a.   Analyze what you've achieved with your first plan.

Modify it, make tweaks, as the music business changes, your plan should also reflect that. Every plan has tweaks made to them.

b.   Put energy & effort into what's working.

Cut off those that are not working for you, you've tried it, it didn't work, release it and move on. It's all about finding things that work for you so you can wash, rinse and repeat.

c.   Create Creative Visuals/Videos

Now that you have a comprehensive idea of your vibe and who you are, your visuals should reflect that. Research creative up and coming directors and see if you vibe. There are plenty of them out there looking to be creative. Try reaching out to some film schools or research the sites where a lot of directors post work for hires.

d. **Make your marketing look cohesive.**
Nothing says "a successful artist" like a well organized marketing strategy and look. From the pictures, to the logo's to the color scheme and theme. When you're in trend, you are relevant and when you are relevant, everyone wants a piece of your action, whether it be licensing, brand collaborations and more… You want to sell records and by having a solid look will help. Most people that scan through iTunes before they hear the record will see your cover. Consumers shop with their eyes and then their ears.

e. **Implement a "Radio Servicing" Strategy**
At this point you should have an idea of what radio wants with respect to your genre. Then it's on you to find you within that trend. You've studied the various record breakers and now it's time to see where your music stack up on the radio.

f. **Service DJ Record Pools**
(Every genre has something that services it.)

Any outlet that you can get your music to gives you every opportunity to win. A Lot of DJ's actually have on air radio shows that they could add your music to. In your specific genre, find out what record pools are servicing it.

(Would be smart to allow some of the dj's of your genre to remix your music, they will play it more and if you've followed the research and registered your music you win either way)

g. **Do Smart Performances**
(Start submitting to festivals)

For festivals, keep in mind that you have to submit to those often a year in advance if they are taking submission

It is time to really expand your brand, your image, your sound, your whole vibe on bigger venues. Your live show should be well rehearsed and as tight as it can be. What is meant by "do smart performances" means that stop paying to be on stages that don't treat you like an artist and or takes you seriously. Get on stages that will definitely help you impact.

SENIORS
The PRO Artist Plan

This is a plan for the Music Release University class geared towards established and artists on the verge- we call them "seniors". The established pro artist plan phase one breaks down like this:

The Pro Artist Plan - This plan is a big budget plan that can transcend the artist into more established areas of the music game. At this point radio knows who you are, and they know what to expect from you. Your next goal is getting on the Billboard Charts and the indicator charts. To achieve that feat, you will need to obtain sales, streams, and views.

As the former pro artist, you have already been in the presence of some radio, you or if you are reading this book to better manage an artist because you or your artist has performed at a few venues or events, now you need "proper radio servicing" to saturate your product. I suggest starting with areas in your warm market and the surrounding areas. I can't stress this enough, you have capture homebase first.

At this time, you must also boost your release, with better visuals, extra marketing support, perform at bigger venues and possibly jump on a tour or start one. The Artist and management should evaluate the analytics of the artist's previous release(s), to gauge where the warm markets are for them and organize a campaign around where the artist is being received well at.

a.   Analyze what you have achieved with your 2nd plan.

Modify it, make tweaks, as success happens, be prepared to add certain things in your plan, especially if momentum is moving quickly.

b.   Put Energy & Effort into what's Working.

Cut off those that are not working for you, you've tried it, it didn't work, release it and move on. It's all about finding things that work for you so you can wash, rinse and repeat.

c.   Create Creative Visuals/Videos

You know who you are, you know what you like and don't when it comes to visuals. Now it's about artistic expression, having the ability to tell a story with your art that resonates with your core audience.

d.   Make sure your Marketing, Stays Consistent.

At this point you have established the layout of your brand and have created a brand identity. Now it's about keeping it consistent and being unique and relevant within the current trend.

e.   Implement a "Radio Servicing" Strategy
If you've done everything right, radio should know you well and now it's about servicing a record that is an undeniable hit. Where it should land you on the charts. Your rollout

matters, radio will more than likely give your song a shot because they know you. For you it's about keeping them there after the fact.

f.   **Service DJ Record Pools**
(Every genre has something that services it.) No explanation needed at this point you should already know the importance of your music being in these pools.

g.   **Festivals and Big Stage Venues**
(Start submitting to festivals and larger stages)

For festivals, keep in mind that you must submit to those often a year in advance if they are taking submission.

You've done enough freemium shows and paid small stage shows at bars and local clubs, now it is time to enter the festival world or big stage shows. Find festivals or larger venues that fit your genre and start applying. All you need is one and then the rest will get wind of your professionalism and entertainment value and invites will begin to roll in.

At this point, you have all the information that is needed and necessary to successfully release your music.

TIMELINES & BENCHMARKS

5. TIMELINES & BENCHMARKS

(Please do not skip to this part and if you did not read the first part of this book and do the exercises, you will only be cheating yourself.)

Now that we have explained university mindsets and outlined the plan for the various mindsets, it's time to add deadlines to your personal plans that you can implement. My rule of thumb is always to give yourself at least 6 to 18 months before your release. I know some of you looked at that timeline right now and were like "whaaat?!, nah bruh, I am releasing my record in 30 days". Hahaha! Well, I say this to say that you will get out of your project what you put into your project, so your 30 days of preparation will only garner the success you prepped for. Now I am not saying that it can't be done, I'm saying it's just highly unlikely given the state of the music industry today, remember, even the quick way has a plan that must be developed if you want to be able to implement it quickly. So, let's jump into what I feel will lead to real success when releasing your record.

15 - 18 MONTHS OUT

This is when the vision happens as well as the research. An artist and or group with or without his or her team, conceptualizes the project, in that 3-month window you should have narrowed down by way of the research, what you would like the project to be based on, understanding the trends and being unique within the trend. It should also reflect the feeling you want it to evoke, the mood and vibe that will help you in your song selections for your project. You should also know where you would like the project to go. You should have your marketing 90% laid out (I only say that because that other 10% will be used to adjust a few things when your project is going to release. You need room to adjust to any unexpected shifts in the music business.)

All the platforms that you are going to appear on should be registered from your "website" to all of the social media platforms, even if there is no artwork and or photos, still go create the pages and as the marketing begins to take shape, then you can add the marketing media to them.

Be sure to register and become a member of a Performing Rights Organization (PRO) both as a "writer" and as a "publisher" so that you can start registering your completed record or album. If you do this as you go along, it will not be overwhelming later as the deadlines approaches.

You should also be recording music at this time. I also suggest discovering who will work and or not work for you, from producers to songwriters (if not you) to the engineers that will be mixing and or mastering your music. Narrow down your team.

11 - 14 MONTHS OUT

By this time, you should have recorded quite a bit of music, best rule of thumb is,

- if you are going to release a 5 song Extended Play (EP) - more than one song more like 3-5 songs), then you should record at least 10 songs and

- if you are going to release an album or Long Play (LP) of 10 songs or more then you should record at least 20 songs or more to ensure that you have the best music that represents the music that you are going to release, the theme, the vibe.

Also, during this time, you should also have your mix and mastering engineer(s) in place that are going to give your music that sonically right sound *(sonically simply means that your music sounds equivalent or better than your competitors in the genre that you choose to be in.)*

You should also start the visuals process to fit the mood, vibe and marketing approach of your ep or lp. Your pictures, your color scheme, your logo's, your "professional bio" *(think about hiring a professional bio writer, a reputable one so that your bio is written properly)* and putting together your talking points.

For the songs you do have, you should have already filled out the "split sheets" and started the registration process for each song that is completed, so that way you are not bombarded at the end when it's time to release and you try to cram everything in, something is bound to be wrong. That's why it's always best to give yourself plenty of time to get everything done.

You should also be studying the competitors in your genre to get an understanding of how they are winning and how you plan to win.

- What is the song structure of their hits?
- What are consumers gravitating to?
- What's happening with their marketing?
- Are these artists moving within the trends?
- What is the radio saying about them?
- What are the media bloggers saying about them? What is making them popular?
- What do their fans like or love about them? (These are likely to be your fans too.)
- What's happening with their marketing?
- How is their live performance?

This is still a part of the "research" and you get a real understanding of what you need to do and or modify in order to be competitive, don't just know about the genre, understand it! Live it, breathe it, be consumed by it to the point that you can not only see the shifts coming, but you will be able to quickly adjust as it happens.

It's time to start putting the finishing touches on your album.

BE READY AND BE IN THE KNOW!

NOTES

07 - 10 MONTHS OUT
GEARING UP FOR THE RELEASE.

At this point you should pretty much have everything laid out for your "rollout". You should now be putting the final touches on your music, mixes and start the mastering process of all of your songs you've prepped for release.

Album/EP/SINGLE artwork should be completed. (The new trend now is "animated Album/EP/Single artwork") definitely, consider that as a part of your rollout. All your marketing assets should have been completed and ready for promotion.

You should have also picked out the single that will represent your vibe and your brand. You should have also started prepping the visuals on top of the artwork. The lyric video should be getting done- written out to submit to lyric websites like Genius. The music video should be prepped, all the tools that are going to be needed to support your release, should be pretty much ready to go with 7 months before the release date.

Your debut and or reintroduction is getting closer and closer.

03 - 06 MONTHS OUT

With 6 months to go before the release of your album or single, it should already be mixed, mastered, and submitted to your distributor for release. You should also have set your pre-sale date, your campaign and promotions to start 3 to

4 months away from your release date to create some anticipation for it.

Through your Spotify™ artist account, you should have submitted your single to Spotify so that you can be considered for some of the verified playlists. *(You must submit your music to Spotify at least 4 to 6 weeks out for it to even be considered playlisting. The earlier the better, it gives the staff plenty of time to review and hopefully select your music to place).* Also, on your personal Spotify account create a playlist(s) that includes your music on it.

At this point verify everything is registered and ready to go. Make sure again that you have all of your split sheets with the one stop clause in it, so you can submit your music for sync licensing simultaneously.

01 - 03 MONTHS OUT

At this point everything should be ready to go, if you have chosen different people to lead your team, check in and make sure all your marketing is ready to go. If it's just you, then "all" of your marketing should be ready to go. Lyric video(s) advertising should be set up to start 30 to 40 days before the release, as it will take at least 3 weeks to 6 weeks to saturate the marketplace. At this point you should have set up interviews via, blog, radio, digital and print media talking about the project, unless you are doing a campaign strictly focused on positioning the record before you do a media run.

Check all sites and platforms that you will be advertising on, and or have write ups on to make sure all your marketing is cohesive and uniformed.

30 days out, start teasing the release of your music on your social media platforms, whether it be a few videos, on TikTok™, Instagram™ and or Facebook™ utilizing your artwork, be creative with it.

Now if you are opting to saturate the record before the social push, then be sure to check every outlet that your music will be distributed to and make sure it's there when the music is released, that way you can troubleshoot the outlets that don't have your music.

You should have your "One Sheet" ready to go, an example will be available in the tools section. The one sheet can be sent to radio, digital, and print media giving them a brief introduction to you and important details on your release.

CONCLUSION

CONCLUSION

In reading "Music Release University: The Indies' Guide to Releasing Music!" I hope that you will be well on your way to becoming the professional recording artist and the superstar that you know you have dwelling in your core. Everybody has the dream and if you've made it this far, then you are one of the rare and few who truly takes this seriously and will more than likely have a solid plan prior to releasing your music.

This industry is constantly evolving. Daily you will hear various song structures, melodies, new platforms that determine who's hot and who's not. Combined with new technology, new trends, new marketing strategies and new business practices It's obvious why artists can be pulled in a lot of directions. Some things are becoming simpler to implement while others have become more complicated. Every artist now has a recording device at their fingertips, a digital distribution outlet, different marketing platforms, etc.... Everything is just a tap and a swipe away with what used to take months and weeks to complete can now be done in mere seconds. Artists are no longer tied to a record label. This is a blessing and a curse because the bulk of the work falls on the artist(s).

As the music industry evolves, so will you. Hopefully we've helped you cultivate your plan and fueled your thirst for knowledge, and my team and I look forward to sharing the master series book or seeing you partake in my on-line course.

If you've learned from this book, feel free to drop us an email and let us know. Also, with this being part of a series and course, my team and I will be digging deeper and sharing more strategies and techniques to help you become more and more familiar with the music industry and what has helped me sustain my career as a professional recording artist, songwriter, and producer.

Thank You!

TOOLS

ARTIST ALBUM / SINGLE RELEASE
CHECKLIST

6 - 18 MONTHS

_____ ESTABLISHED A VISION
_____ DID THE RESEARCH
_____ OUTLINED YOUR GOALS
_____ CREATED A MARKETING PLAN
_____ UNDERSTAND YOUR BRAND
_____ WROTE AND CREATED SOME
       AWESOME MUSIC
_____ REGISTERED WITH A PRO
       (BMI, ASCAP or SESAC)
_____ GET YOU YOUR OWN ISRC NUMBER
_____ REGISTERED ON ALL SOCIAL MEDIA
       and FREEMIUM MUSIC PLATFORMS
_____ TOOK SOME GREAT PHOTOS
_____ CREATED A WEBSITE
_____ CREATED A SOLID BIO
_____ CREATED UNIQUE ALBUM / SINGLE
       ARTWORK
_____ CUSTOMIZED YOUR MARKETING
       ROLLOUT
       (Banners, Flyers, Web Banners and
       Campaigns)
_____ CREATED AN EPK (Electronic Press Kit)
_____ REGISTERED YOUR MUSIC | SIGNED
       UP FOR THEMUSICRC.com
_____ REGISTERED THE COPYRIGHTS
_____ REGISTERED AND UPLOADED YOUR
       MUSIC ON SOUNDEXCHANGE
_____ GOT YOU AN ISNI NUMBER
_____ CLAIMED ARTIST ACCOUNTS
       (Spotify, Apple Music, and more)
_____ CREATED A PLAYLIST PLAN

_____ SUBMITTED YOUR LYRICS ONLINE
_____ CREATED A MOVING VISUAL FOR SONG
_____ CREATED A LYRIC VIDEO
_____ CREATED A MUSIC VIDEO
_____ HAVE AN ALBUM RELEASE DATE
_____ HAVE A DIGITAL AGGREGATOR
_____ CREATE A "ONE SHEET"
_____ ESTABLISHED AN EMAIL LIST
_____ SENT OUT A NEWSLETTER ANNOUNCING YOUR RELEASE.
_____ HAVE A PLAN TO INCREASE YOUR FANBASE CONGRATULATIONS, YOU'RE READY TO RELEASE!
_____ CONTACTED A RADIO SERVICING COMPANY
_____ CONTACTED A PUBLIC RELATIONS COMPANY
_____ WIKIPEDIA (have to be notable for this)

New artists keep in mind there is levels to having a publicist!

LINKS

ISRC (The International Standard Recording Code)
www.usisrc.org

What is an ISRC for a song?
The International Standard Recording Code (ISRC) system is the international system for the identification of recorded music and music videos. Each ISRC is a unique identifier that can be permanently encoded into a recording or music video that is released by you as an artist and or label.

THE MUSIC REGISTRATION COMPANY
(The MRC)
www.themusicrc.com

PRO'S
(Performing Rights Organization)

BMI
(Broadcast Music, Inc.)
www.bmi.com

ASCAP
(American Society of Composers, Authors and Publishers)
www.ascap.com

SESAC
(Society of European Stage Authors and Composers)
With SESAC you must be invited to join.

SOCAN
(Society of Composers, Authors & Music Publishers of Canada)
www.socan.com

GEMA
(Georgian Society of Authors & Composers Germany)
www.gema.de

REGISTER YOUR LYRICS

GENIUS.COM
www.genius.com/

LYRICS.COM
www.lyrics.com/

AZLYRICS
www.azlyrics.com

LYRICSMODE
www.lyricsmode.com

DIGITAL DISTRIBUTION PLATFORMS

TUNECORE
www.tunecore.com

DISTROKID
www.distrokid.com

CD BABY
www.CDBaby.com

UNITEDMASTERS
www.unitedmasters.com

NECTAR
www.nectardistro.com

RECORD UNION
www.recordunion.com

SPINNUP
www.spinnup.com

AWAL
www.awal.com

LEVEL
www.levelmusic.com

MUSIC VIDEO DISTRIBUTION

YANGAROO
www.yangaroo.com

DISTROVID
www.distrovid.com

SYMPHONIC
www.symphonic.com

COVER ART DESIGNERS

FIVRR
www.fivrr.com

WE MAKE THE BRAND
www.wemakethebrand.com

CANVA
www.canva.com

ADOBE
www.adobe.com

POSTER MY WALL
www.postermywall.com

Although a lot of these companies give you templates, you can customize them to what you need.

SONGWRITING TOOLS

THESAURUS
www.thesaurus.com

DICTIONARY
www.dictionary.com

RHYMEZONE
www.rhymezone.com

THESAURUS
www.thesaurus.com

MASTER WRITER
www.masterwriter.com

SUGGESTER: CHORDS AND SCALES
Apple App Store

SCALES-CHORDS
www.scales-chords.com/chordid.php

RHYME BRAIN
www.rhymebrain.com

SPLIT SHEET TEMPLATE WITH ONE STOP

(You can either copy this format given to you or you can go to this website a one stop resource center for all of your registration needs, as well as some freemium tips too www.TheMusicRC.com and download it)

NAME:
ARTIST:
SONG TITLE:
GENRE:
LENGTH:
TEMPO:
DESCRIPTION:

WRITER #1
Full Legal Name (includes middle initial):

_____
Gender: _____
Date of Birth: _ _ / _ _ / _ _ _ _
Social Security, Social Insurance or Tax ID #:
_____
Performing Rights Society Affiliation:
(ASCAP, BMI or SESAC): _____
Performing Rights Society IPI/CAE Name
Number: CAE/IPI No.:

[WRITER]
(__%) #_____   _____
                IPI NUMBER   WRITER'S NAME

[PUBLISHING]
(__%) #_____   _____
                IPI NUMBER   PUBLISHERS NAME

Phone#:_____

Mobile Phone: _____

Email address:

_____

Address:

_____

_____

City: _____ State: _____

Zip: _____

WRITER #1
Full Legal Name (includes middle initial):

_____
Gender: _____
Date of Birth: _ _ / _ _ / _ _ _ _
Social Security, Social Insurance or Tax ID #:

_____
Performing Rights Society Affiliation:
(ASCAP, BMI or SESAC): _____
Performing Rights Society IPI/CAE Name
Number: CAE/IPI No.:

[WRITER]
(__%) #_____ _____
        IPI NUMBER WRITER'S NAME

[PUBLISHING]

(__%) #_____ _____
         IPI NUMBER PUBLISHERS NAME

Phone#:_____

Mobile Phone: _____

Email address:

_____

Address:

_____

_____

City: _____ State: _____

Zip: _____

WRITER #3
Full   Legal   Name   (includes   middle   initial):

_____

Gender: _____
Date of Birth: _ _ / _ _ / _ _ _ _
Social Security, Social Insurance or Tax ID #:

_____
Performing Rights Society Affiliation:
(ASCAP, BMI or SESAC): _____
Performing Rights Society IPI/CAE Name
Number: CAE/IPI No.:

[WRITER]

(__%) #_____ _____
         IPI NUMBER WRITER'S NAME

[PUBLISHING]

(__%) #_____ _____
        IPI NUMBER PUBLISHERS NAME

Phone#:_____

Mobile Phone: _____

Email address:

_____

Address:

_____

_____

City: _____ State: _____

Zip: _____

Note: IF THERE ARE MORE THAN THREE WRITERS, JUST ADD ANOTHER ROW UNTIL YOU'VE INCLUDED ALL WHO WAS INVOLVED IN THE WRITING PROCESS, PRODUCERS INCLUDED.

ONE STOP CONTACT:

NAME: _____

PHONE: _____

EMAIL _____

We have agreed to and have given _____
_____ the right to
individually sign off and clear any and all Non-
Exclusive sync licensing (publishing) and / or
master use licensing (sound recording) deals on
behalf of all songwriters, publishers and master
owners involved.

_____
can absolutely and immediately authorize 100%
clearance and represent the record non-
exclusively as "ONE STOP"

1. Income derived from any and all sources
   (i.e. streaming, downloads, licensing, etc)
   will be split according to percentages noted
   above.

   _____
   will distribute records to any and all DSPs
   (iTunes, Spotify). Once the first sync or
   master use licensing placement has been
   secured. Any monies collected shall be split
   as agreed upon and % portions forwarded
   within 30 days of receipt.

2. If any samples are contained in the
   Composition for which the sampled
   writer(s) / publisher(s) are to receive a
   copyright interest in and to the composition,
   then we agree that the producer(s)
   songwriters and publisher shares in the
   copyright and / or monies attributable to the
   Composition shall be reduced
   proportionately.

**** Confidentiality Statement ****

The information contained in this document(s) contains confidential information intended for a specific individual(s) and purpose, and is protected by law. Disclosure of any of the confidential information contained in this document, is unauthorized and subjected to legal action.

Agreed to by:

NAME:_____ aka_____

X_____ Date: _____

NAME:_____ aka_____

X_____ Date: _____

NAME:_____ aka_____

X_____ Date: _____

ONE SHEET TEMPLATE:

Your one sheet should include the following: Artist Logo, Street Date, UPC Label, Artwork, Description of the album or single, Sounds Like, Artist Info, Track Listing if its an album, Marketing Points, Song/Album Credits, Social Media, Contact & Label Logo.

STREET DATE
JAN. 14, 2022
#859750260680

8 59750 26068 C

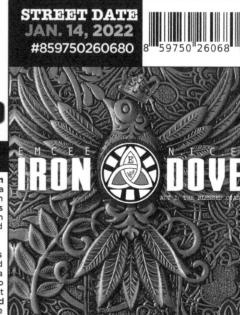

"Even though Emcee N.I.C.E., who really is "nice" on the mic, isn't a household name as of yet, he soon will be!"
- GlobalGrind.com

Emcee N.I.C.E. returns with his sophomore CHH album **"Iron Dove - Act I: The Blessed Coast"**, the first installment from a follow up trilogy to his hit debut Christian Hip Hop Album "Praise" that garnered him with a number 1 album on Billboard's "Top Gospel Album" chart as well achieving number 1's on Billboard's Digital Gospel chart and Top 10's on the Billboard Christian chart.

With the "Iron Dove" three act trilogy, Emcee N.I.C.E. sets his sights on bridging the gap between Christian/Gospel and CHH/Gospel Rap with a story that follows the journey of a heroic messenger sent by God to assemble a spiritual army to fight the demonic enemies, share the gospel and bring about harmony, unity and peace among his people. Act I: The Blessed Coast is the Iron Dove's arrival to the west coast aka "The Blessed Coast" where he is tasked with assembling the army for the war, 19:19 (Act II).

Iron Dove is musically brought to life by super producers, **Sam Peezy, Lamontt Blackshire** & **Marv4MoBeats** and has an ensemble of Legends in gospel such as **Fred Hammond, Bishop Cortez Vaughn,** Hip Hop Legend **Domino,** Gospel Rap Legend **ChilleBaby** of the **GospelGangstaz,** Gospel chart toppers **Uncle Reece & Sam Peezy** along with newcomers *Erica Mason, Jessica Hitte, J. Will, Rezurrection, Jarrett Burton, DaLomonze* & Billboard chart topper **Alonda Rich.** The album is mixed by multi-platinum Engineer, Grammy nominated **Ray Seay** of Atlanta *(Flo Rida, Pitbull, T.I., Snoop Dogg, Rick Ross, Lil Jon)* & Mastered by Grammy Nominated Chief Mastering Engineer **KennyMixx** *(Dr. Dre, Kanye West, Pitbull, Blanco Brown, Rick Ross, T.I., 2Chainz, Lil Wayne).* Executive Produced by **Aulsondro "Novelist" Hamilton, Christopher Starr** of **CSP Music Group** & **Chantal Grayson.**

Sounds Like:

2 PAC
50 CENT
KANYE WEST
JAY Z

Artist: Emcee N.I.C.E.
Title: IRON DOVE (Act I) [The Blessed Coast]
Label: Gypsy City Music
Release Date: January 14th, 2022
Genre: Christian/Gospel Hip-Hop/Rap
UPC: #859750260680

TRACK LISTING:
01. IRON DOVE (Act I) - The Arrival [Opening] - (1:10)
02. FOR THE GLORY (feat. Phil J) - (2:57) ★
03. THE BLESSED COAST - (3:32)
04. THE G IN ME (feat. Domino, Rarebreed & Chillebaby of the Gospel Gangstaz) - (3:45)
05. KING MODE - (3:32)
06. ALL MY LIFE (feat. Uncle Reece) - (3:46)
07. THAT'S ON ME (feat. Sam Peezy & Rezurrection) - (3:34)
08. IRON DOVE (Act I) - Tell The Others [Interlude] - (1:30)
09. ROCK THE BODY (feat. Alonda Rich) - (3:44) ★
10. GIVIN GLORY (feat. Fred Hammond) - (3:54)
11. IS IT REAL? (feat. Erica Mason x J. Will) - (3:37)
12. YEAH (feat. Jarrett Burton) - (4:45) ★
13. THE WAY (feat. Jessica Hitte) - (3:56)
14. LIFT ME UP (feat. Bishop Cortez Vaughn) - (4:01)
15. DANCIN (feat. DaLomonze) - (3:19)
16. FREE (feat. J. Will) - (3:51)
17. IRON DOVE (Act II) - [19:19 The War] [outro] - (1:36)

Executive Producers:
Aulsondro "Novelist" Hamilton, Christopher Starr & Chantal Grayson

Producers: Sam Peezy, Marv4MoBeats & Lamontt Blackshire
Mixed by: Ray Seay @ Studio Seay (Atlanta, GA)
Mastered by: KennyMixx @ Son Pur Audio (Atlanta, GA)

MARKETING POINTS
- Key Targeted Markets
- Targeting All National & Local TV Outlets (Christian, Gospel & Secular)
- Major Print Press
- Service DJ Pool
- Service Radio (P-1, Digital, P-2 & College Stations)
- Targeted Strategic Online Promotions (FB, YT, IG, TW & more...)
- 12 to 24 City Tour (TBA) & Festival Headliner
- Promotional Tour & Guest Appearances in Key Target Markets
- Motion Picture Release

@EmceeNICELA   /EmceeNICEMusic   @EmceeNICELA

AVAILABLE FOR INTERVIEWS

CONTACT
@GMAIL.COM

www.EmceeNICE.com

ACTUAL SIZE 8.5 11INCHES

86

ABOUT THE AUTHOR

To be a catalyst, one would have to cause change and that change would disrupt the norms to create new norms. This is often a part of one's evolution. For almost 30 years, Aulsondro "Novelist" Hamilton also known as Emcee N.I.C.E., a veteran Hip Hop artist, producer, writer, and all-around creative, has been constantly evolving in both music and leadership. His body of work includes collaborations with rap icons NAS and 2Pac (posthumously), a song on the soundtrack Academy Award-winning film "Crash," a cover of a Prince song, enthusiastically approved by The Artist himself. 17 number #1 records on the Billboard, BDS, iTunes & Amazon music charts and in the fields of Gospel & Christian, he is the recipient of a Stellar Award and several Gospel Spin Awards including being honored as "Radio Man of Year" in 2021. Aulsondro is the Co-creator of the urban animated series "Da Jammies," the first African American animated music series to appear on Netflix for kids. N.I.C.E. knows no creative limits.

His introduction in gospel music and Christian rap, came with his debut album "Praise" and single "I Got Angels". This project garnered him five-time #1 Billboard Inspirational Christian Hip Hop Gospel star by chart-topping Billboard sales and airplay as the #1 Top Gospel Albums, #1 Gospel Album Sales, #1 Hot Single Sales, and #1 Digital Song Sales.

As amazing as the songs are, the emergence of Emcee N.I.C.E., on multiple charts measuring independent albums, Christian songs, R&B/Hip-Hop albums, and emerging and current artists has placed him in rare air as a notable trailblazer coming from secular to gospel music. Emcee N.I.C.E. turned loose a boutique unorthodox marketing team that devised a "digital street team strategy" combined with grassroots analytics and a robust database to propel his music and brand, connecting directly to the culture and influencers.

Music, Ministry, and Message are at the heart of Emcee N.I.C.E.'s divinely inspired artistry - the hallmarks of a life and career steeped in purpose and service.

Aulsondro Hamilton was born to a Black father and a Puerto Rican mother in Los Angeles, California but raised from first grade to his sophomore year of high school in El Paso, Texas. His mother named him "Aulsondro" which means "prosperous protector of the reflection of light." Growing up most of his life in a single parent household, he was touched by the work ethic and leadership of his mother who toiled at three jobs (bartender, K-Mart manager, and creator of unique and stunning wall art made from thumb tacks and yarn) to provide for him and his little brother in 2002 his brother was murdered and his mother passed away in 2021.

At a young age, he and his brother started a rap duo, turning shopping carts from the corner store into a stage in their apartment building where they rocked the mic for candy. As he matured, Aulsondro embraced the style and power of Hip Hop, especially groups like RunDMC, Boogie Down Productions, Brand Nubians and Rakim, plus backpack era/daisy age such as De La Soul.

He was also galvanized by Christian Rap, especially Soldiers For Christ associate member Poetic Lee. "That's when I realized it was cool to talk about God in music," N.I.C.E. shares. "He returned back to California to enroll in Bible College at CWFC in Pasadena. After embarking upon independent study of comparative religions via books and querying some often-befuddled ministers - N.I.C.E. came to the conclusion that the common denominator is, simply, God.

Taking the stage name "Novelist" (he'd been writing short stories since childhood which dovetailed into rap rhymes), Aulsondro co-formed the "urban rock" duo KansasCali which made a name in Hollywood as a strong entity for movie soundtracks including the Oscar-winning "Crash,"

"Mr. & Mrs. Smith" and "Once in a Lifetime" (a biopic on soccer giant Pele') and Jamie Kennedy's, "Kicking It Old Skool" where their song features as the end title.. KansasCali became a band and eventually changed its name to The Rocturnals and scored with "This is Where Amazing Happens" that was adopted as the official theme song of the NBA All-Star 2010. The group was also invited by keyboardist Matt "Dr." Fink of Prince's band to contribute a cover of a Prince song to a tribute CD. Their take on "Pop Life" was signed off on immediately by The Artist himself who called it one of the best Prince covers ever.

If it feels like there is no end to the goals and dreams of Emcee N.I.C.E., that's the point. He'll likely have to create a new title to replace the limiting "Emcee." His vision and mission are epiand Praise-worthy.

NOTES

NOTES